BEARING WITNESS

GENOCIDE AND ETHNIC CLEANSING IN THE MODERN WORLD™

THE RWANDAN GENOCIDE

ZOE LOWERY and FRANK SPALDING

ROSEN PUBLISHING
NEW YORK

Published in 2017 by The Rosen Publishing Group, Inc.
29 East 21st Street, New York, NY 10010

First Edition

Library of Congress Cataloging-in-Publication Data

Names: Lowery, Zoe, author. | Spalding, Frank, author.
Title: The Rwandan genocide / Zoe Lowery and Frank Spalding.
Other titles: Bearing witness (Rosen Publishing Group)
Description: New York : Rosen Publishing, 2017. | Series: Bearing witness | Includes bibliographical references and index.
Identifiers: LCCN 2015050277 | ISBN 9781477785706 (library bound)
Subjects: LCSH: Genocide—Rwanda—Juvenile literature. | Ethnic conflict—Rwanda—History—20th century—Juvenile literature. | Rwanda—History—Civil War, 1994—Atrocities—Juvenile literature. | Rwanda—Ethnic relations—History—20th century—Juvenile literature.
Classification: LCC DT450.435 L69 2016 | DDC 967.5710431—dc23
LC record available at http://lccn.loc.gov/2015050277

Manufactured in China

CONTENTS

INTRODUCTION

In 2015, a walk through Kigali, Rwanda's capital, shows almost no sign of the horrors that so recently came close to crippling the African country. Although Rwanda is one of the poorest countries in the world, Kigali's streets are clean and safe. It's so safe that people can walk alone at night. Few African countries can make that claim. But just over twenty years ago, the scene was gravely different. A three-month killing spree changed the country forever.

Countless piles of skulls offer devastating evidence of the atrocities that occurred during the Rwandan genocide.

The Second World War (1939–1945) is well known as the twentieth century's most devastating armed conflict. Nations all over the globe joined one side or the other. The Allied Powers were made up of Britain, Canada, and the United States, and the Axis Powers encompassed Germany, Italy, and Japan. The Allies would ultimately claim victory but not before more than seventy million people had died.

Although the war had no shortage of tragedies, at its conclusion some of the most brutal news was revealed: Nazi Germany had attempted to methodically annihilate specific groups of people, including the handicapped, homosexuals, and political enemies, as well as ethnic groups including Roma (gypsies) and Jews. Jewish people were intensely victimized. By the end of the war, somewhere around six million of them had been ruthlessly slaughtered.

It was a systematic process. The Nazis forced people to go to concentration camps, where they had no choice but to suffer through backbreaking work. Those who didn't starve to death died as a result of illness or were outright killed. The word *genocide* was coined in 1943 to describe this systematic killing of the Jewish people.

Promises echoed from all over the world: these atrocities would never happen again. With fervent hopes that no such worldwide clash would happen in the future, in 1945 a worldwide organization was founded to promote international peacekeeping and collaboration: the United Nations (UN). Fifty-one members joined that first year, and as of 2015, nearly two hundred countries count themselves among the member states of the United Nations.

On December 11, 1945, the first version of the United Nations' Convention on the Prevention and Punishment of the Crime of Genocide was written. It formally took effect in 1951. It includes a worldwide accepted definition of genocide, which is "acts committed with intent to destroy, in whole or in part, a national, ethnical, racial, or religious group." Among the actions that can be included under this definition are murder, imposing circumstances that would obliterate a people, or endeavoring to stop them from having the ability to have or rear offspring.

In spite of the best intentions of the international community, since the Second World War, several genocides have ensued. In the tiny but populated Rwanda, a ghastly genocide started on April 6, 1994, and lasted through the middle of July of that same year. Although it lasted just one hundred days, almost a million people had been slaughtered by the time it ended.

The butchery was fast and cruel—often occurring with clubs or machetes—and executed under the eyes of UN peacekeeping force. Worldwide, politicians were fully aware of the cruelties in Rwanda, but they failed to help. And when they finally acted, it was too late. Hundreds of thousands of adults and children had brutally lost their lives.

CHAPTER 1

RWANDA'S MODERN HISTORY

Rwanda is a tiny country in the middle of Africa. Although the population exceeds twelve million, the people there are very poor.

In the middle of Africa, there is a tiny country called Rwanda. It covers about 10,000 square miles (25,900 square kilometers), which means it is just almost the same size as the U.S. state of Maryland. The countries of Burundi, the Democratic Republic of the Congo (formerly known as Zaire), Tanzania, and Uganda surround Rwanda. More than twelve million people call this country home, making it Africa's most densely populated nation. Kigali, the capital, in and of itself is home to more than one million people. Meanwhile, this country is extremely poor; most Rwandans live on less than $1.50 a day. Most make that little bit of money through subsistence farming. Exports of tea and coffee keep the economy afloat together with increased tourism.

THE PEOPLE OF RWANDA

The people that settled Rwanda thousands of years ago farmed and raised cattle. Over time, a sort of aristocracy of powerful people arose. These people eventually became known as the Tutsi, a word that was originally used to refer to someone who owns a lot of cattle. Everyone who was not a Tutsi became a Hutu.

Generally, the Tutsi tended to have lighter complexions and to be tall and slender, while the Hutu tended to have darker complexions and be stockier. But the supposed differences in ethnicity or appearance between Hutu and Tutsi were, for all intents and purposes, eliminated by intermarriage between the two groups.

There were many more Hutu than Tutsi in Rwanda. The population of Rwanda was about 90 percent Hutu and 10 percent Tutsi. A third group of people, the Twa, who were hunter-gatherer Pygmies, made up less than 1 percent of the population. All Rwandans shared the same religion and partook of the same culture. In the past, Rwanda was a monarchy ruled by a king. Even today, though horribly and violently divided, all Rwandans speak the language Kinyarwanda, and many also speak Swahili. French and English are also spoken by some.

COLONIAL RULERS

Dr. Heinrich Albert Schnee was the last governor of the African territory known as German East Africa.

Ultimately, Rwanda's future would be shaped by European colonialism. Colonialism is the practice of a powerful nation extending its reach by dominating another nation or people. Beginning in 1885, European colonial powers established control over the majority of African nations. When the colonial powers divided up control of the continent, borders were established that typically ignored the existing divisions between different African regions, ethnic groups, and kingdoms.

German colonists arrived in Rwanda in the late nineteenth century. But after Germany's defeat in World War I (1914–1918), it lost control of Rwanda, which then fell under Belgian control. Belgium altered Rwanda's government by placing Tutsis—and only Tutsis—in positions of power. The Belgians believed that Tutsis had more "Caucasian" features than Hutus and were therefore more fit to rule. Blatantly racist beliefs such as these were common in Europe at the time.

First, however, the Belgians had to determine exactly who was a Hutu and who was a Tutsi. This was a difficult proposition at best. The boundary between the two groups of Rwandans was not fixed: Hutus could become Tutsis and vice versa. The Belgians required every Rwandan to register him- or herself as a Hutu, Tutsi, or Twa. This now made it nearly impossible for a Hutu to become a Tutsi, or vice versa. The population was, quite literally, divided. Beginning in 1933, the Belgians issued ethnic identity cards that everyone was required to carry. Later on, ethnic identity cards would prove to have disastrous consequences for a large portion of the Rwandan population.

A POPULATION DIVIDED

The Belgians used Tutsis to help them run the country. In return, Tutsis were granted distinct advantages. They received better educations than Hutus and were also largely exempt from the kind of manual labor that was the Hutus' lot in life under Belgian rule. In fact, Tutsis were used by the colonists to oversee and manage Hutus engaged in forced labor.

The Hutus' work was so fatiguing that many of them, exhausted by a day of backbreaking work, were too tired to tend their own crops. This resulted in massive famines. Eventually, some Rwandans fled to other countries, hoping they would be able to make a better living abroad.

Over the years, the Hutu began to resent the special status granted to the Tutsi. Many began to view the Tutsi in the same way they saw the colonists: as oppressors.

King Kigeli V Ndahindurwa, the last monarch of Rwanda, was exiled in 1961 when Rwandans voted to get rid of the monarchy.

FIGHT FOR INDEPENDENCE

By the middle of the twentieth century, a continent-wide movement had begun for African independence. This movement gained popularity in Rwanda, especially among the Hutu. They were tired of being second-class citizens within their own country.

In 1959, an uprising that would become known as the Hutu Revolution began. The Hutu wanted to gain greater control over Rwanda. Violence broke out, and hundreds of people lost their lives before peace was restored. The fighting was only a precursor to major changes that would occur. In an effort to quell further conflict, the Belgians replaced a number of Tutsi administrators with Hutus. Then, in 1961, Rwandans voted to abolish their monarchy.

Tutsi rebels mounted a failed invasion of Kigali in 1963. They had a force of several hundred but were defeated before they could even reach Kigali. The Hutu retaliation against Tutsi civilians was quick and brutal. Between the end of December 1962 and early January 1963, thousands of Tutsis were killed, including men, women, and children—anyone who was carrying a Tutsi identity card. More than 200,000 Tutsis fled the country, joining the swelling ranks of Tutsi Rwandan exiles.

POPULATION IN EXILE

During the Hutu Revolution, approximately 10,000 Tutsis fled the country to live a life of exile. However, they did not forget where they came from and wanted to return. A good portion of these Tutsi exiles stuck together and formed a fighting force. They began launching periodic attacks on Rwanda's Hutu leadership. However, the Tutsi forces in exile were not strong enough to regain control of the government. Hutu "hard-liners"—or those Hutus with extreme political beliefs—sometimes used these attacks to turn public sentiment against the Tutsi.

In 1967, eight years after the Hutu Revolution had begun, 300,000 more Tutsis were forced into exile. For the time being, exiled Tutsis stopped launching attacks. Within Rwanda, extremists killed 20,000 Tutsis simply for being Tutsi. Rwanda's Tutsi minority began facing discrimination in areas such as employment.

Throughout all of these political changes, the rigid ethnic classification established by the Belgians persisted. Rwandans knew if their friends and neighbors were Hutu or Tutsi. Tutsis who did not leave Rwanda sometimes figured out ways to have their ethnicity reassigned to become Hutu. By 1991, the Tutsi population was less than half of what it was prior to the Hutu Revolution.

CHAPTER 2

THE TWISTED TRAIL TOWARD GENOCIDE

When Juvénal Habyarimana, the general of the Rwandan army, took power in 1972, the future of Rwanda began a frightening new course. His plan for Rwanda was executed through the formation of a political party known as the National Revolutionary Movement for Development (MRND), which would become Rwanda's sole political party before long.

When Rwandan army general Juvénal Habyarimana became president in 1972, the country veered in a horrifying direction.

JUVÉNAL HABYARIMANA

After reinventing the nation as a one-party state, Habyarimana went about consolidating his power. Because there was no party opposing him, he, in effect, had the support of the entire country's population. Under Habyarimana, the people of Rwanda were forced to participate in manual labor projects designed to maintain Rwanda's roads and land. Improvement of Rwanda's public infrastructure attracted foreign investment, giving the country's economy a boost.

Among his supporters, Habyarimana enjoyed especially strong support from Rwanda's army and police force. Rwanda had an army known as the Forces Armeés Rwanda (FAR), which included a police force. The police force was known as the Gendarmerie. In addition to this, Habyarimana had a special elite force directly under his command, known as the Presidential Guard. Habyarimana's Presidential Guard had upward of a thousand members. All three groups, and their loyalty to their president, would play a key role in the genocide to come.

TUTSI REFUGEES

Once Habyarimana became president, organized attacks against Tutsis were effectively brought to an end, although discrimination against them continued. This relative peace didn't mean that Tutsis living abroad were welcomed home, however. Citing Rwanda's chronic overpopulation problem, Habyarimana refused to allow any Tutsi exiles to return to Rwanda. In fact, he even forbade the friends and family members of the exiles from visiting them in the countries where they were living.

The exiles survived as best they could as refugees. In Uganda, for instance, thousands of exiled Tutsis were welcomed into the Ugandan army, where they distinguished themselves as soldiers. Using the training they'd received, they would eventually form their own highly disciplined military organization, called the Rwandan Patriotic Front (RPF).

SHAKY ECONOMY

It seemed that conditions in Rwanda were steadily improving. True equality had not yet been achieved between the Hutu and Tutsi, and overpopulation was still a problem, but the economy was improving. Foreign investors were eager to put their money into Rwanda. Its main exports, tea and coffee, were selling well.

After tea and coffee values plummeted in 1986, Rwanda's exports were no longer bringing in much-needed income and the people relied on foreign aid.

Things changed dramatically in 1986, when the value of tea and coffee dropped drastically. Suddenly, Rwanda's main exports were no longer very profitable. These economic problems affected the entire population, Hutu and Tutsi alike. Soon, many people were struggling to survive—and the president was losing support.

More than half of Rwanda's income was now provided by foreign aid. Widespread corruption swept the country, as various political and business figures scrambled for economic control. At the same time, in response to international pressure, Habyarimana reluctantly loosened his autocratic control over Rwanda. For the first time in years, opposition parties were allowed to have a token public voice. The Habyarimana regime was not eager to relinquish power, and democracy did not suddenly flourish in Rwanda. Repression against those who dared oppose the government continued.

Habyarimana could not afford to become unpopular among Rwandan Hutus. They were his core supporters. He was also wary of the threat presented by the quarter million Tutsi exiles living just beyond the Rwandan border.

ANTI-TUTSI PROPAGANDA

In October 1990, the first RPF invasion of Rwanda took place. Several hundred RPF Tutsis attacked Rwanda but were held off by the army. France and Belgium, longtime supporters of the Habyarimana government, sent troops and weapons to assist in the fight against the RPF.

The Habyarimana regime knew it could control the people of Rwanda by blaming the country's problems on a common enemy: the RPF. Extremist factions within the regime began spreading negative propaganda about Tutsis. For instance, they began funding an anti-Tutsi newspaper. This paper published articles on how the Tutsi, as an ethnic group, were supposedly dangerous. It also published the names of Rwandans who were supposedly criminal collaborators with the RPF. Many people were listed who had nothing at all to do with the RPF—their names may have appeared on the list because they opposed the current regime or had simply angered someone in power. Denouncing a Tutsi, or even a Hutu with moderate political views, as being a "traitor" to Rwanda would become a common practice.

"THOSE WHO STRIKE AS ONE"

Habyarimana's party, the MRND, had an organization for young people called the Interahamwe, which loosely translates into "those who strike as one." The Interahamwe would soon become one of the most violent factions in the nation. Its thirty thousand young, mostly poor members were fed a steady diet of anti-Tutsi propaganda and false promises. The Interahamwe promised new recruits that they would get money, food, and perhaps even the homes and land of Tutsis they killed. As a result, they became Hutu extremists. They wore brightly colored red, green, and black shirts—the same colors as the Rwandan flag. Soon, they began carrying weapons such as machetes and wooden clubs. They also began compiling the names and addresses of Tutsis.

KIBUYE BLOODBATH

Anti-Tutsi sentiment erupted in 1992, when a horrific massacre took place in the city of Kibuye, Rwanda. Tutsis were also killed in the area south of Kigali and in the city of Gisenye, which is on the border Rwanda shares with the Democratic Republic of the Congo (which was then known as Zaire). The killings were triggered by a fictitious report from the government claiming that the RPF was planning to kill a large number of Hutus. There was absolutely no element of truth to this report—the whole thing had been made up simply to provoke violence against Tutsis. Moderate Hutus, many of whom were political enemies of the regime, were also targeted. Hundreds of innocent people were killed.

In late 1993, the situation was no better. French troops had to protect these civilians from armed Hutus as they waited for food from relief agencies.

MORE BRUTALITY

Tensions were ratcheted up again on October 21, 1993. In the neighboring country of Burundi, the democratically elected president, Melchior Ndadaye, was assassinated. Ndadaye, a Hutu, was killed by RPF soldiers. The RPF tried to assert control over Burundi, but it was driven back by Hutu forces. This failed coup ended with the deaths of thousands of Burundi Tutsis at the hands of Burundi Hutus. In retaliation, Tutsis killed Hutus.

Like Rwanda, Burundi had a population made up of Hutu, Tutsi, and a small number of Twa. Approximately 300,000 people, mostly Hutu, fled Burundi after Ndadaye's death. They came to Rwanda as refugees. Hutu organizers entered the refugee camps and recruited heavily from among the Hutu refugees living there.

A PEACE AGREEMENT

After the killings, the Habyarimana government and the RPF declared a truce. They agreed to end the violence and the killings and signed a formal peace agreement on August 3, 1993. This agreement was known as the Arusha Accords, named for the city of Arusha, Tanzania, where it was signed.

The Arusha Accords were intended to end the violence against the Tutsis and halt the anti-Hutu RPF attacks. The accords stripped Habyarimana of much of his power, transferring it to an interim Rwandan government. This government would now allow members of the RPF to participate and engage in debates. RPF troops were supposed to be integrated into the FAR. The accords also guaranteed Rwandan exiles the right to return to their country.

Not everyone was a fan of the Arusha Accords, especially Habyarimana himself. Having held power in Rwanda for about twenty years, he was not anxious to relinquish it. Even though he lost a lot of his direct power over state affairs, Habyarimana retained the fanatical support of Hutu hard-liners.

Those responsible for the killing of Tutsis, however, were never brought to justice. The government had no intention of punishing anti-Tutsi murderers. Hutu groups like the Interahamwe quickly realized that there would be no legal repercussions for any crimes they might commit against Tutsis.

PEACE IN PERIL

The United Nations sent a small peacekeeping force to Rwanda, under the leadership of Jacques-Roger Booh-Booh from Cameroon. The mission's force commander was General Roméo Dallaire from Canada. The mission was entitled the United Nations Mission in Rwanda (UNAMIR) and was initially comprised of over two thousand troops. The UN troops were primarily there to enforce the conditions of the Arusha Accords and to act as a deterrent to violence by reminding the nation's leaders that all the world was watching what happened in Rwanda.

But on November 18, 1993, only a few months after the Arusha Accords had been signed, violence broke out again. This time, twenty-one people were killed, and the murders were blamed on the RPF. However, UN observers were not so sure and reserved judgment. Hutu extremists took this to mean that the UN supported the Tutsis.

The relentless propaganda of the Hutu Power extremists, which was not only published in newspapers but also broadcast continually on their own radio station, Radio Télévision Libre des Mille Collines (RTLMC), had succeeded in completely dividing the country. They relentlessly spread hatred against Tutsis, calling them *inyenze*, or cockroaches. There was no longer any room for political moderates or middle ground of any sort. Anyone who wavered in his or her support for the Habyarimana regime was branded a traitor.

President Juvénal Habyarimana died when his plane was shot down on April 6, 1994. The culprits were never discovered.

TRIGGERING THE GENOCIDE

On April 6, 1994, the plane President Juvénal Habyarimana was traveling in was shot down, and he was killed. The Hutu president of Burundi, Cyprien Ntaryamira, also died in the crash. To this day, no one knows who is responsible for shooting down the plane. Some think that it was the RPF, while others believe it was Hutu extremists who were upset that Habyarimana had signed the Arusha Accords.

The RPF denied that it had anything to do with Habyarimana's death, but it was blamed for it all the same. As soon as the news got out, ethnic violence exploded all over Rwanda. After a focused campaign of killing, which lasted around one hundred days, the country would never be the same again.

CHAPTER 3

ABSOLUTE HORROR: RWANDA'S GENOCIDE

General Roméo Dallaire (shown here in 2015) sent faxes to the UN regarding information about Interahamwe militia training.

The horrors of the genocide in Rwanda may have lasted just one hundred days, but between 800,000 and one million people died in a matter of months. These deaths hardly happened on the sly—governments from across the globe as well as the United Nations were kept abreast of what was going on. Despite knowing all about the atrocities going on, the world did no more than watch and listen. Rwanda was left to fend for itself.

HINTS AT THE HORRORS TO COME

On January 11, 1994, months before Habyarimana was killed, General Roméo Dallaire sent a fax to UN headquarters in New

York City. The fax outlined information provided to UNAMIR from a Hutu informant who was in charge of training Interahamwe militia members. Although he could be killed if anyone found out he was talking to the UN, the informant refused to stand by while innocent civilians were killed.

The fax contained a startling amount of information about the violence that was about to engulf the country. The informant had told General Dallaire that Hutu extremists were planning to provoke the RPF into attacking them, in the hopes of breaking the Arusha Accords and creating a civil war.

Hutu Power extremists were also hoping to provoke the Belgian soldiers who were part of the UNAMIR force. Their plan was to get the Belgian soldiers to use a display of force first. Then, Hutu hard-liners would counterattack and kill several Belgian soldiers. If this sequence of events unfolded, the Hutu extremists were convinced that Belgium would withdraw its troops from Rwanda. The Belgians were among the best-trained, best-equipped soldiers on the UNAMIR force.

General Dallaire's fax also detailed testimony from the informant that directly linked the FAR, the Interahamwe, and the Gendarmerie. Two thousand members of the Interahamwe were being trained in fighting techniques by the FAR. The informant believed that the Interahamwe was registering every single Tutsi in the country in order to be able to quickly, efficiently, and systematically exterminate the entire Tutsi population. In addition, he identified the location where the extremists were keeping their weapons. Everything mentioned in the fax would come to pass in the months that followed.

THE STRUGGLES OF ROMÉO DALLAIRE IN RWANDA

General Roméo Dallaire was born in 1946 and raised in Montreal, Canada. Dallaire rose through the ranks of the Canadian army, eventually attaining the rank of brigadier-general. In 1993, the UN picked Dallaire to be the force commander of its peacekeeping mission in Rwanda. Initially there to implement the Arusha Accords, Dallaire watched the genocide unfold in front of his eyes. His requests for more money and additional troops were ignored by the United Nations. During the early 1990s, UN peacekeeping disasters in Somalia and the former Yugoslavia made UN member nations hesitant to intervene for peacekeeping purposes.

Dallaire stayed in Rwanda with a woefully small force of dedicated peacekeepers, trying to help those that he could. At the very least, he could bear witness to the events of the genocide. In August 1994, the stress became too much for Dallaire, and he asked to be relieved of his command. In 2000, he retired from the Canadian army. In 2004, Dallaire returned to Rwanda to testify against Colonel Théoneste Bagosora, one of the architects of the genocide. Since the genocide, Dallaire has continued to be active in international politics.

In exchange for all of this information, General Dallaire's informant wanted protection for himself and his family. He knew that if his identity was discovered, he would be killed. Dallaire asked the UN for permission to raid the extremists' weapons cache and to provide the informant with protection.

The UN responded that these requests went beyond the parameters of the mission. The UNAMIR troops were allowed to use force only if they were attacked directly. As a result, over the one hundred days of the genocide, UN troops would stand idly by and be unable to stop the killing of Tutsis going on all around them.

UNBRIDLED HATRED

The names and addresses of nearly every one of Rwanda's Tutsis had been recorded. After Habyarimana's death, Tutsis were methodically hunted down and killed. The names and addresses of Tutsis were also read out over RTLMC radio. While the killers went from door to door, slaughtering innocent people, the Interahamwe set up a series of roadblocks all over Kigali. Those attempting to drive through the city would be stopped at the roadblock and forced to present their identification cards. If they were Tutsi, they would be killed, often after being horribly tortured first.

The first people targeted in the genocide were moderate Hutu and Tutsi politicians who had not already fled or been killed. Nearly every single one of these officials was dead by April 7, 1994, the day after Habyarimana's plane was shot down.

Also on April 7, Hutu extremists captured ten Belgian UNAMIR soldiers. RTLMC had spread the rumor that the Belgians and the Tutsis were both complicit in the assassination of the president. The captured Belgians were executed. Playing directly into Hutu hands, Belgium prepared to withdraw its soldiers from the UNAMIR force.

A Rwandan Patriotic Front (RPF) solider fires his weapon in April 1994.

Many members of the RPF had family living in Kigali or other Rwandan towns and cities. For many of them, it was too difficult to maintain a cease-fire while their relatives were being killed or were under imminent threat of being killed. Therefore, the RPF attacked, violating the terms of the cease-fire that had already been ruptured by Hutu extremists and the army and police forces. The FAR responded in kind, and civil war erupted in Rwanda.

FLEEING RWANDA

By April 9, 1994, foreign nationals in Rwanda were being evacuated from the country. France and Belgium sent military forces to transport their citizens to safety. By April 12, everyone had been evacuated, and the Belgians had withdrawn from UNAMIR. By April 15, it became clear that the UN would not send any additional troops to halt the growing genocide.

The remaining UNAMIR force was very weak. It did not have enough soldiers or weapons to stop the killing by force even if the UN had allowed it to do so by expanding the parameters of its mission. According to General Augustin Bizimungu (a colonel in the FAR who was promoted to general the day after Habyarimana was killed), the genocide was being committed by rebel factions beyond his control. But with no leader in Rwanda exerting himself to check the power of the Hutu extremists, the FAR, Interahamwe, and Gendarmerie no longer attempted to conceal the fact that they were all working together in their efforts to exterminate the Tutsi population.

INVOLVEMENT: ENFORCED AND VOLUNTARY

Before the genocide began, not every Hutu in Rwanda was an extremist. The FAR, Gendarmerie, Interahamwe, and other militia groups made up a relatively small percentage of the Hutu population. But by the end of the genocide, a large percentage of the Hutu population had participated in the killings.

This participation could have been as simple as reporting that one's neighbors were Tutsi or as extreme as helping staff a roadblock where Tutsis were detained and killed. RTLMC ceaselessly urged all Hutus to take up arms against the Tutsis, who were called traitors and cockroaches. The killers were men, women, and even children from all walks of life. Most of the killing was done with clubs and machetes, and Tutsi victims were often tortured and mutilated. Women were often raped before being killed. No one was spared during the slaughter, not even children or pregnant women.

Young Hutu militiamen trained to fight with the Rwandan government against the RPF rebels in 1994.

Not every Hutu was willing to kill. But those who refused to kill were often branded as traitors, a crime punishable by execution. Some Hutus who showed reluctance to take part in the genocide were forced to kill their neighbors. In such cases, a member of an extremist faction, such as the Interahamwe, would give them a club or a machete and tell them to kill. If they hesitated, or refused, they themselves would be killed on the spot.

Avoiding the slaughter was often a matter of luck more than anything else. Some Tutsis managed to maneuver past the roadblocks and roving bands of killers and escape to safety. Others managed to somehow hide themselves until the violence had ended. There were also a few very brave Hutus who used their authority, influence, or wits to help those Tutsis that they could. But the Rwandan genocide was a well-organized atrocity, and it was nearly impossible to escape it.

METHODICAL MASSACRE

The genocide was organized on each and every level of Rwandan society. Organizers included politicians, members of the military, and businesspeople. The genocide would never have occurred if these people hadn't meticulously planned and carefully directed it.

Colonel Théoneste Bagosora, the former leader of Habyarimana's Presidential Guard, was instrumental in provoking the genocide. He was close to Agathe Habyarimana, the widow of the former president. Agathe Habyarimana was herself part of the Hutu extremist movement's inner circle, known as the *akuza* (which means "little house").

Prior to President Habyarimana's death, Bagosora was instrumental in the creation of the Interahamwe. He helped train them, transforming the young soldiers into a lethal fighting force. He also directed these young people in intelligence activities such as gathering information on Tutsis. Bagosora realized that there were not enough weapons in Rwanda to conduct a genocide, so he ordered that more weapons be imported.

Military commander Anatole Nsengiyumva supervised the Interahamwe between June 1993 and July 1994.

The Rwandan government broadcast propaganda on RTMLC radio that encouraged people to take part in the violence. But in some areas in southern Rwanda, Hutus and Tutsis lived together in peaceful, fully integrated communities. In the early days of the conflict, many Hutus banded together with their Tutsi neighbors and friends. Interahamwe militias were instrumental in spreading the violence in the south, forcing Hutus to participate in the killing of their Tutsi friends and neighbors.

The existence of the Interahamwe also allowed those in power to distance themselves from the mass killings. Despite the fact that the army trained and directed the Interahamwe and other groups, they remained separate entities. When confronted by the UN, Hutu authorities could claim that the Interahamwe was composed of extremist factions that were acting independently.

The police force of Rwanda did nothing to stop the genocide. In fact, the police went door to door with members of the Interahamwe or FAR soldiers, slaughtering Tutsis. Early in the killing, Tutsis trying to save their lives begged the Gendarmerie to save them. Instead of protecting all Rwandans, which was

This photograph shows the remains of just some of the four hundred Tutsi victims who were killed in a church on September 16, 1994.

their duty, the Gendarmerie killed Tutsis or brought in others to kill them.

Traditionally, churches have been places where people in trouble can go to seek sanctuary and escape harm. In Rwanda, this was not the case. The first episode of genocide witnessed by UNAMIR was at Gikondo Parish Church. On April 9, the Gendarmerie rounded up hundreds of Tutsi men, women, and children and brought them to the church. They then collected everyone's identification cards. The Gendarmerie invited militiamen into the church, and these soldiers killed every single Tutsi inside.

After the massacre, the identification cards of those killed were burned by the Gendarmerie. They also destroyed the official records of each person killed in an attempt to erase these individuals from existence.

APPEARANCES CAN BE DECEIVING

The government tried to maintain the appearance of normal life during the genocide. People still went to work, and children still went to school. The government, police, and militias were all complicit in the genocide, and there were no media outlets criticizing what was going on. RTLMC often used coded language when promoting the genocide, such as telling listeners to "crush cockroaches." Announcers also often referred to the killing as "work" and reminded listeners to have their "tools" at hand.

Now, when Hutus gathered to take part in their obligatory work detail, such as building roads or clearing brush, they were instead expected to seek out and kill Tutsis. Religious leaders called community meetings, but the topic of conversation would not be love, peace, or brotherhood. Instead, it was extreme anti-Tutsi propaganda. Businesspeople did their part by donating money to the army, which was collecting for a "self-defense fund." The nature of this fund was not clearly defined, but the donated money went directly to the soldiers participating in the killing.

The efficiency of the killing during the Rwandan genocide is unparalleled in modern history. Never have so many people been killed so quickly. Prisoners were sent out to pick up the corpses filling the streets, homes, churches, and schools in Rwanda and load them into garbage trucks. Dogs roamed the streets of Kigali, feasting on the bodies of the dead.

A GRADUAL END TO GENOCIDE

Meanwhile, the RPF, under the leadership of Rwanda's future president, Paul Kagame, made slow but steady progress against the FAR forces. Although they were outnumbered, members of the RPF benefited greatly from their superior training, discipline, and leadership. They captured more and more territory until, in July 1994, they occupied Kigali.

The city they took over was devastated. There were dead bodies everywhere, and buildings had been extensively looted. The sewage system was destroyed, and vandals had tainted the drinking water. There was no fuel, electricity, or phone service. And because the crops had gone unharvested for months, food was scarce.

The genocide had come to an end, but the violence did not stop right away. Now that the RPF controlled Kigali, a series of retribution murders against Hutus took place. About two million Hutus fled the country. The great majority ended up in Zaire (today known as the Democratic Republic of the Congo). It is believed that many of those who left had a hand in the killings. Living off of international aid in large refugee camps, they regrouped and kept their organization largely intact.

Paul Kagame (pictured in July 1994) trained the RPF before he became the country's president.

CHAPTER 4

SURVIVORS' STORIES

Everyone in Rwanda was affected by 1994's horrific events. Not only was 10 percent of the population killed, but of all Tutsis inhabiting Rwanda as the genocide raged on, only a mere one quarter lived. Just about every person knew another who had either participated in killing or who had been killed. Rwandans of all ages had to watch as someone they knew was killed. Each Rwandan genocide survivor has a terrifying tale to share.

MASSACRE AT NYARUBUYE CHURCH

Nyarubuye Roman Catholic Church was the site of one of Rwanda's worst massacres. It is located in the province of Kibungo, sixty miles (ninety-six kilometers) east of Kigali. After Habyarimana was killed, Tutsis fled to the church, seeking sanctuary. The mayor of the town was a Hutu man named Sylvestre Gacumbitsi. He was the one who had told the Tutsis

The Nyarubuye Roman Catholic Church has been transformed from a site of unthinkable horrors to a genocide memorial.

that they would be safe in the church. Less than ten days after Habyarimana was killed, Gacumbitsi led the police, as well as thousands of armed Hutus, to the church.

The killers told the Tutsis that they could buy their freedom. But after they handed over their money, they were killed anyway. Grenades were tossed at the Tutsis hiding in the church, and they were shot at. Then the killers moved in with clubs and machetes, killing anyone who still survived inside. The bodies piled up, and blood was everywhere. Those inside begged for their lives or tried to fight back. However, they had no weapons. If they tried to escape, they were killed. The slaughter took so long that the killers had to work in shifts. Many of the slayers slept outside the church at night, only to resume killing the next day. It took them four days before they were finished.

There were thousands of Tutsis hiding in the church—some estimates run as high as ten thousand or even twenty thousand. Nearly every person in the church was killed. Those who survived managed to hide themselves among the bodies of the dead.

One of these survivors, a woman named Flora Mukampore, pretended to be dead. The killers found her and hit her in the head with a hammer, but still she lived. Mukampore hid among the bodies for an entire month, even after they had begun to badly decay. A thirteen-year-old girl named Valentina also survived by hiding among the bodies. She had been struck on the head and hand with a machete, but it did not kill her. Like Flora, she hid in the church, not coming out for forty-three days.

It was incredible that Flora and Valentina managed to survive such extreme brutality against such grim odds. Like all survivors, however, their lives would be changed forever. Valentina's family had been killed, and Flora lost seventeen family members. The Nyarubuye Church is now a monument to those who died there.

The church memorial includes an exhibit made up of the very bones and clothes of the victims who died in the massacre there.

SAFE HAVEN IN THE HOTEL

Paul Rusesabagina was a Rwandan hotel manager who managed to save over a thousand people from being killed during the genocide. Rusesabagina was a Hutu of mixed parentage (his father was a Hutu, his mother was a Tutsi). His wife, Odette Rusesabagina, was a Tutsi, and they had four children.

Sabena Hotels, a Belgian company that had hotels in Kigali, employed Rusesabagina. Beginning in 1984, he worked for Sabena at the Hôtel des Mille Collines, eventually becoming its manager.

Rusesabagina would remain the manager of the Hôtel des Mille Collines until July 1994. During this time, he would use every resource at his disposal to protect himself, his family, and every single person who came to the hotel seeking refuge from the horrors occurring outside.

Rusesabagina had a number of resources at his fingertips that were not available to the average Rwandan. Some prominent extremists had Tutsi relatives or

Hotel owner Paul Rusesabagina offered every resource he had to Tutsis who needed a safe place during the genocide.

wives. They left them at the hotel during the genocide, believing this to be the safest place for them. It was therefore in their best interest that the hotel not be attacked. Rusesabagina bribed people with the money held in a safe in the Hôtel des Mille Collines. The hotel had a large stock of alcohol, which he also used to bribe people. Most of these bribes were simple—in one way or another, Rusesabagina convinced the killers to leave the hotel in peace. And as it filled up, more and more lives were on the line.

The Hôtel des Mille Collines was known to everyone in Kigali. Even though Rusesabagina was harboring Tutsis, important Hutus involved in the genocide would visit the hotel for drinks or to collect bribes. The fate of the hotel was completely at their mercy.

The people being sheltered in the hotel remained there for months. After the water supply was cut off, they used the water in the hotel's swimming pool. Rusesabagina had a lot of business contacts from his years working in the hotel business, and he took full advantage of them during the genocide. Rusesabagina arranged to procure alcohol to replace the hotel's stocks, depleted by all the bribes offered to Hutu soldiers. He also arranged for food to be delivered to sustain the hotel's growing number of refugees.

The hotel also had a special phone line that was used for its fax machine. Because it was separate from the hotel's other phone lines, it remained unaffected when they were cut. With this one phone line, Rusesabagina began making calls and sending faxes to anyone he thought might be able to help.

Actor Don Cheadle portrayed Paul Rusesabagina in the film *Hotel Rwanda,* which tells the story of his good deeds during the genocide.

A very small UNAMIR force had been stationed outside the hotel, but it was not strong enough to repel a large-scale attack. On May 3, UNAMIR attempted to evacuate some of the refugees, including Rusesabagina's wife. There were sixty-two refugees in all, headed for the airport. They were offered asylum by the Belgian government. However, the evacuation did not go unnoticed. News of the convoy was brought to RTLMC. The radio station immediately broadcast a warning to all listeners that there was a convoy of Tutsis trying to escape. With bloodthirsty mobs blocking their way, the convoy was forced to return to the hotel.

The RPF was steadily capturing more territory. If the people in the Hôtel des Mille Collines could find a way into RPF-controlled territory, they would be safe. On June 18, 1994, they did just that. UNAMIR escorted Rusesabagina and his family, along with all of the people they'd worked so hard to protect, to safety. The Rusesabagina family now lives in Belgium, where Paul owns a trucking company.

STRUGGLE TOWARD SAFETY

Not everyone was lucky enough to find his or her way to the Hôtel des Mille Collins. For those Tutsis stranded among roving bands of drunken, machete-wielding Interahamwe members, staying alive was often just a matter of luck.

Eleven-year-old Hamis Kamuhanda watched members of the Interahamwe break into his house and drag his father off into the night. They fired indiscriminately into the Kamuhanda house, and Hamis pretended to be dead. To make sure he wasn't faking, one of the killers cut off his leg with a machete.

Hamis survived the attack. His mother and siblings did, too. Besides Hamis, none of them were gravely wounded. They could not risk trying to head for a hospital, and instead hid in the house until the RPF came. Had the RPF not managed to seize control of Kigali, and eventually the entire country, it's possible that every last Tutsi left in Rwanda would have been killed.

CHAPTER 5

A PEACEFUL FUTURE

Rwanda was faced with a daunting mission after the genocide. It had to rebuild its economy, infrastructure, government, and society. No one knew how Hutus and Tutsis would be able to coexist without conflict after the horrors of the genocide. The only sure thing was that Rwanda's future would be peaceful.

JUSTICE

An entirely new government needed to be established in Rwanda. This new government was multiethnic, consisting of both Tutsis and Hutus. The new president of the country, Pasteur Bizimungu, was a Hutu, as were the prime minister and the majority of the government's cabinet members. Paul Kagame, a Tutsi and former leader of the RPF, became vice president and defense minister. He was elected president in 2003.

When a new Rwandan government was built, Paul Kagame became vice president and minster of defense before he was elected president in 2003.

Approximately two million Hutus fled Rwanda after the RPF took control of the country. They lived in large refugee camps outside of Rwanda's borders. Hutu Power exiles regrouped there, recruiting new members and preparing to return to Rwanda when they were strong enough. Kagame launched an attack on the Democratic Republic of the Congo, where the largest refugee camps were, in order to force the refugees to return to Rwanda. There, they would be beholden to

About two million refugees poured into refugee camps in search of a safe place for their families.

Rwandan law and would be imprisoned or reintegrated into society. Violence in the region sparked a new war that resulted in nearly four million deaths.

The new Rwandan government was faced with the problem of how to ensure that justice was served. The government estimates that about two million Hutus played a role in the genocide. It was clear that not every single killer could be caught and punished.

Instead, the government began arresting those who had a hand in organizing and promoting the genocide. They then went after the more notorious killers. Rwanda's prisons soon filled up with those who participated in the genocide. Prison overcrowding became a major problem: if every Hutu who killed a Tutsi during the genocide was given a prison sentence, there would not be room for them all in Rwandan jails. Another problem was that safety could not always be guaranteed for those who testified against the killers. Many survivors of the genocide have been killed as a result of their testimony. As it stands, about 500 people have been executed for their role in the genocide, and more than 100,000 were imprisoned.

Punishing the killers was only one obstacle for post-genocide Rwanda to overcome. A more pressing challenge was learning to live together as a nation once again. Hutus and Tutsis had lived side by side in the same neighborhoods before the genocide, and they did so again afterward. Even if forgiveness might not have been possible right away, people had to learn at least to get along. There has been a concerted effort to bring people together, but violence and division have not yet been eliminated from Rwanda.

FROM EXILE TO PRESIDENCY

Paul Kagame was born in southern Rwanda in 1957. His family went into exile in 1959, and he grew up as a refugee in Uganda. As a young man, Kagame gravitated toward military life. He formed the RPF in 1985. Kagame distinguished himself as a master tactician during the genocide. The superior discipline of the RPF troops allowed them to claim victory over the Hutu extremists. Kagame has been criticized for not allowing dissenting political opinions to exist in Rwanda or allowing true freedom of the press. According to Kagame, this is to prevent his opponents for spreading divisive racial rhetoric.

VICTIMS ON BOTH SIDES

Tutsis were not the only victims of the genocide. Many Hutus were killed as well. Some of them were killed for political reasons, and most of these killings happened early on in the genocide. But others were killed for a great number of reasons. Some were accused of being Tutsis simply because they looked like Tutsis. Personal enemies killed others. So many people were being killed during the hundred days of the genocide that it was easy literally to get away with murder.

Those who survived the genocide still have many difficulties to overcome. Many people were physically mutilated during the genocide and have had to learn to live with their handicaps. Many others suffer from psychological problems such as post-traumatic stress disorder. The genocide also deprived many children of their parents, and there are thousands upon thousands of orphans in Rwanda today.

It is believed that anywhere between 250,000 and 500,000 women were raped during the genocide. Most of the women who were raped were also killed. Life has not been easy for the survivors. Approximately 70 percent of these rape victims contracted the HIV virus, which was prevalent in Rwanda. Rwanda is an impoverished country, and it's rare that those with HIV can afford the expensive drug treatments that would keep them healthy and alive. Many female victims had children fathered by the rapists, which they then had to raise alone. They also had to live with the social stigma that their status as rape victims conferred upon them, and many were essentially ostracized by their communities.

TAKING RESPONSIBILITY

Perhaps no one person can be directly blamed for the genocide. But many different people and groups share some of the responsibility for it. There are the killers and the organizations that helped them operate, such as the Interahamwe. There are the businessmen that imported weapons such as machetes, knowing full well what they would be used for. There are the government leaders who led the killers to the Tutsis in their communities. There are the people who encouraged violence, such as the staff of RTLMC radio, and those in the Hutu extremist movement.

The responsibility even extends beyond the borders of Rwanda, encompassing a number of international entities that either supported the killers or refused to stop the violence. For instance, the French supplied the Habyarimana regime with the weapons used to kill Tutsis.

In this age of instantaneous communication and media saturation, it is impossible for foreign powers to claim that they were not informed about the Rwandan genocide. What happened in Rwanda happened in full view of the entire world. The simple fact is that no one wanted to get involved. Had the relatively small force General Dallaire asked for been granted to him, it would have sent a message to the extremists that the world would not tolerate a ruthless mass murder. Instead, the international community ignored what was happening or refused to admit that it was actually a genocide. Once they admitted a genocide was occurring, they would have been bound by the UN to help stop it, and they did not want to contribute the money or troops to do so.

The killers knew that while powerful Western nations might claim to be committed to ending genocide, they would not involve themselves in a part of the world in which they had no political or economic stake. It seems that, in Rwanda, the only thing at stake was human life. Apparently, that wasn't enough.

DECADES LATER

A decade after the genocide, there are monuments all over the country to those who were killed. Former U.S. president Bill Clinton has apologized for his reluctance to use U.S. force to intervene in the genocide. Kofi Annan, the head of UN Peacekeeping Operations during the genocide, has also accepted his share of responsibility for failing to prevent the genocide.

At a 2004 service marking the ten-year anniversary of the genocide, President Kagame made a speech about the events of a decade before. Addressing a capacity crowd in a Kigali stadium, he told them, "We cannot turn the clock back nor can we undo the harm caused, but we have the power to determine the future and to ensure that what happened never happens again." At the 2014 twenty-year anniversary, the country was still healing its deep scars. But according to the *New York Times,* Kagame announced, "Today we have a reason to celebrate the normal moments of life, that are easy for others to take for granted. If the genocide reveals humanity's shocking capacity for human cruelty, Rwanda's choices show its capacity for renewal."

Even more than twenty years later, ethnic tensions are still evident in Rwanda. As of 2015, 93 people have been indicted by the UN International Criminal Tribunal for Rwanda (ICTR) for participating in Rwanda's 1994 genocide.

While it may be some time until Rwanda's situation is stabilized, its economy is strengthening. Though not without his critics, Kagame works tirelessly to make Rwanda self-sufficient and to reduce its dependence on foreign aid. Hopefully Rwanda is headed toward a future characterized by understanding and compromise. Hopefully the world has gained valuable insight, too, about the importance of stepping up when innocent lives are at stake.

TIMELINE

1918 Belgium assumes control of Rwanda. Tutsis are used to control the population of Rwanda and are shown favoritism.

1926 All Rwandans are issued ethnic identity cards labeling them as being Hutu, Tutsi, or Twa.

1959–1962 There is a Hutu uprising against the Tutsi and Belgian colonists. Hutus win a great number of government elections. Thousands of Tutsis flee the country, fearing for their lives.

1962 Rwanda achieves its independence from Belgium. The Belgian colonists withdraw from the country.

1963 A force comprised of Tutsi exiles sweeps into Rwanda, launching an attack on their home country. Hutus carry out reprisal killings against Tutsis living in Rwanda. These killings continue sporadically for the next ten years.

1973 General Juvénal Habyarimana becomes president of Rwanda. Discrimination against Tutsis persists, but violence against them largely ceases before resuming in the early 1990s.

1986 The RPF is formed. It will eventually come under the command of Rwanda's future president, Paul Kagame.

OCTOBER 1990 An RPF force, numbering a few hundred, invades Rwanda. They are eventually repelled.

1992 The Kibuye Massacre occurs.

1993 The RPF launches attacks on Kigali.

AUGUST 3, 1993 The Arusha Peace Accords are signed in Arusha, Tanzania. The UN sends troops to ensure that they are carried out.

NOVEMBER 18, 1993 Violence breaks out as twenty-one innocent people are killed. Their deaths are blamed on the RPF, although there seems to be evidence to the contrary.

JANUARY 11, 1994 Roméo Dallaire sends a fax to UN headquarters, detailing how the Hutu extremist movement is stockpiling weapons and preparing to commit violent acts against UN soldiers and innocent Tutsis. The UN does not approve Dallaire's proposed plan of action.

APRIL 6, 1994 The plane carrying Rwandan president Juvénal Habyarimana and Cyprien Ntayamira, the president of Burundi, is shot down by unknown assailants.

APRIL 7, 1994 The genocide begins.

APRIL 8, 1994 UNAMIR soldiers see the first evidence of mass murder of Tutsis at the Gikondo Parish Church.

APRIL 12, 1994 All foreign nationals are evacuated from Rwanda.

APRIL 21, 1994 The UN withdraws the majority of its troops from Rwanda, leaving behind only a small force of a few hundred.

JULY 1994 The genocide against Tutsis is effectively brought to an end when the RPF captures the city of Kigali. Sporadic killings still occur throughout the country.

DECEMBER 1996 Trials begin for those accused of participating in the genocide.

2003 Paul Kagame is elected president of Rwanda.

2004 The ten-year anniversary of the genocide is reached.

2005 Major Hutu rebel group announces plans to end its armed struggle.

2010 Kagame is reelected.

2014 The twenty-year anniversary of the horrific genocide still finds people healing.

2015 As of 2015, the UN International Criminal Tribunal for Rwanda has indicted 93 people for participating in Rwanda's 1994 genocide.

GLOSSARY

annihilate To completely destroy, eliminate, or defeat.

aristocracy A group of rich and powerful people, often born into their positions of privilege. In monarchies, aristocrats are given a large role in the functioning of a government.

colonialism The practice of a powerful country conquering a less powerful region, establishing political control over it, and exploiting it to extract wealth and resources.

concentration camp A location where large groups of people, such as minorities or political prisoners, are confined and imprisoned under harsh conditions, sometimes waiting for extermination. It often includes Nazi extermination camps.

ethnicity A distinctive group set apart from others by a common culture, language, or place of origin.

exterminate To kill every single member of a group of humans or animals.

genocide The organized and systematic attempt to destroy a group of people completely, through murder or other means.

hard-liner A person who adheres to a strict and sometimes extreme set of beliefs.

Hutu Power A movement based on the ideas that Hutus ought to support each other and oppose other ethnic groups.

Interahamwe A militia group, made up of largely disaffected young Hutus, who were the foot soldiers of the genocide. Their name means "those who strike as one" or "those who stand together."

Nazi A shortened name for the National Socialist Party that ruled Germany during World War II. All other political parties were outlawed in Germany from 1933 to 1945. Led by Adolf Hitler, the Nazi Party established a racist, anti-Semitic, homophobic state that aimed to conquer as much of Europe as possible and to subjugate or exterminate races it considered inferior.

obliterate To remove completely all traces of something; to destroy.

peacekeeping Military missions in which international troops try to prevent violence between two warring groups, keep the peace, or bolster law and order in war zones. It may also involve humanitarian work, human rights monitoring, and assistance in honoring the terms of a peace agreement.

propaganda Media created to influence people's views. Negative propaganda is often used to turn public sentiment against a group of people or political party.

Pygmy A member of a group of people who are quite short in height and who live in parts of Africa and Asia.

recruit To find new members for a group, such as a political party or army.

subsistence farming Farming practiced by individual households, which usually provides just enough food to feed one family over the course of a year.

United Nations (UN) An organization created to promote peace, stability, economic cooperation, and security around the world.

FOR MORE INFORMATION

American Red Cross National Headquarters
2025 E Street NW
Washington, DC 20006
(703) 206-6000
Website: http://www.redcross.org

The Red Cross is an international humanitarian organization that was founded in 1881. The American Red Cross is part of the International Red Cross, which provides humanitarian aid and disaster relief to afflicted regions of the world.

Amnesty International USA
5 Penn Plaza
New York, NY 10001
(212) 807-8400
Website: http://www.amnestyusa.org

Amnesty International is the largest human rights organization in the world. It works to safeguard and promote human rights around the world. It is a nonprofit, nongovernmental institution and has been awarded the Nobel Peace Prize.

Doctors Without Borders /Médecins Sans Frontières (MSF)
333 7th Avenue
New York, NY 10001-5004
(212) 679-6800
Website: http://www.doctorswithoutborders.org

Founded in 1971, Médecins Sans Frontières (MSF), known in English as Doctors Without Borders, is a nongovernmental organization that provides medical aid to countries that need it. The organization is active in nations facing widespread disease or that have suffered through war and violence.

Human Rights Watch
350 Fifth Avenue, 34th Floor
New York, NY 10118-3299
(212) 290-4700
Website: http://www.hrw.org
Human Rights Watch was established in 1978 to safeguard human rights. It is a nongovernmental organization that extends its efforts to ninety countries around the world.

Oxfam America
226 Causeway Street, 5th Floor
Boston, MA 02114

1101 17th Street NW, Suite 1300
Washington, DC 20036-4710
(800) 776-9326
Website: http://www.oxfamamerica.org
Oxfam America is one of seventeen countries that are part of the international Oxfam confederation, a nongovernmental organization that works to find solutions to human rights abuses, famine, poverty, and injustice in more than ninety countries around the world.

United Nations Headquarters
First Avenue at 46th Street
New York, NY 10017
Website: http://www.un.org
The United Nations was founded in 1945. Headquartered in New York, the UN works to bring nations together to mediate international disputes and promote peace and stability throughout the world.

WEBSITES

Because of the changing nature of Internet links, Rosen Publishing has developed an online list of websites related to the subject of this book. This site is updated regularly. Please use this link to access the list:

http://www.rosenlinks.com/BWGE/rwanda

FOR FURTHER READING

Burnet, Jennie E. *Genocide Lives in Us: Women, Memory, and Silence in Rwanda* (Women in Africa and the Diaspora). Madison, WI: University of Wisconsin Press, 2012.

Carr, Rosamund Halsey. *Land of a Thousand Hills: My Life in Rwanda*. New York, NY: Plume, 2014.

Combres, Élisabeth. *Broken Memory: A Novel of Rwanda*. New York, NY: Groundwood Books, 2011.

Kayihura, Edouard, and Kerry Zukus. *Inside the Hotel Rwanda: The Surprising True Story ... and Why It Matters Today*. Dallas, TX: BenBella Books, 2013.

McKenna, Amy. *The History of Central and Eastern Africa* (The Britannica Guide to Africa). New York, NY: Rosen Publishing, 2011.

Meredith, Martin. *The Fate of Africa: From the Hopes of Freedom to the Heart of Despair*. Rev. ed. New York, NY: Public Affairs, 2011.

Nardo, Don. *The Rwandan Genocide* (World History Series). Detroit, MI: Lucent Books, 2011.

Reader, John. *Africa*. Rev. ed. Washington, DC: National Geographic Society, 2007.

Rusesabagina, Paul, and Tom Zoellner. *An Ordinary Man: An Autobiography*. London, England: Bloomsbury Publishing, 2014.

Shillington, Kevin. *History of Africa*. Third ed. New York, NY: Palgrave Macmillan, 2012.

BIBLIOGRAPHY

Amanpour, Christiane. "Looking Back at Rwandan Genocide." CNN.com. April 6, 2004 (http://edition.cnn.com/2004/WORLD/africa/04/06/rwanda.amanpour/index.html).

BBC News. "Eyewitness: A Survivor's Story." April 2, 2001 (http://news.bbc.co.uk/2/hi/africa/1252049.stm).

BBC News. "Rwanda Country Profile—Overview" June 4, 2015 (http://www.bbc.com/news/world-africa-14093238).

BBC News. "Rwanda Profile—Timeline." June 25, 2015 (http://www.bbc.com/news/world-africa-14093322).

BBC News. "UN Admits Rwanda Genocide Failure." April 15, 2000 (http://news.bbc.co.uk/1/hi/world/africa/714025.stm).

Cowell, Alan. "20 Years After, Rwanda Pauses to Recall Carnage." *New York Times,* April 7, 2014 (http:/www.nytimes.com/2014/04/08/world/africa/genocide-commemorations-begin-in-rwanda-with-curtailed-french-role.html?_r=0).

Dallaire, Roméo A., and Brent Beardsley. *Shake Hands with the Devil: The Failure of Humanity in Rwanda*. New York, NY: Carroll & Graf Publishers, 2004.

Fischer, Ian. "Hutu and Tutsi Ask: Is a Unified Rwanda Possible?" *New York Times,* April 6, 1999 (http://www.nytimes.com/1999/04/06/world/hutu-and-tutsi-ask-is-a-unified-rwanda-possible.html).

Gettleman, Jeffrey. "The Global Elite's Favorite Strongman." *New York Times*, September 4, 2013 (http://www.nytimes.com/2013/09/08/magazine/paul-kagame-rwanda.html?_r=0).

Goodman, Walter. "Young Witness to Rwanda Massacre." *New*

York Times, April 1, 1997 (http://query.nytimes.com/gst/fullpage.html?res=9B07E7DD1E3AF932A35757C0A961958260).

Gourevitch, Philip. *We Wish to Inform You That Tomorrow We Will Be Killed With Our Families: Stories from Rwanda.* New York, NY: Picador USA, 1998.

Human Rights Watch. *Leave None to Tell the Story: Genocide in Rwanda.* March 1999 (http://www.hrw.org/reports/1999/rwanda/index.htm#TopOfPage).

Human Rights Watch. "Rwanda: Killings Threaten Justice for Genocide." January 22, 2007 (http://hrw.org/english/docs/2007/01/19/rwanda15126.htm).

Keane, Fergal. "Deliver Us from Evil." *Independent,* April 3, 2004 (http://findarticles.com/p/articles/mi_qn4158/is_20040403/ai_n12785209).

Lacey, Marc. "10 Years Later in Rwanda, the Dead Are Ever Present." *New York Times*, February 26, 2004 (http://query.nytimes.com/gst/fullpage.html?res=9401E3DB133CF935A15751C0A9629C8B63).

Lorch, Donatella. "Heart of Rwanda's Darkness: Slaughter at a Rural Church." *New York Times*, June 3, 1994 (http://query.nytimes.com/gst/fullpage.html?res=9A0DE0DE1E3BF930A35755C0A962958260).

Prunier, Gérard. *The Rwanda Crisis: History of a Genocide.* New York, NY: Columbia University Press, 1995.

United Nations. "Statement on Receiving the Report of the Independent Inquiry into the Actions of the United Nations During the 1994 Genocide in Rwanda." December 16, 1999 (http://www.un.org/News/ossg/sgsm_rwanda.htm).

INDEX

ABOUT THE AUTHORS

Zoe Lowery is an avid student of history, constantly reading and studying about the past and other thought-provoking topics. She has written and edited a number of books for Rosen Publishing. Lowery lives in Colorado.

Frank Spalding is a writer based in New York State. He has had a lifelong interest in politics and international affairs.

PHOTO CREDITS

Cover (photo) Chip Somodevilla/Getty Images; cover (cracked texture) Marbury/Shutterstock.com; p. 4 kamnuan/Shutterstock.com; p. 7 Rainer Lesniewski/Shutterstock.com; p. 9 Hulton Archive/Getty Images; pp. 11, 18, 37, 39 © AP Images; p. 13 Universal Images Group/Getty Images; pp. 15, 21, 27, 32 Scott Peterson/Hulton Archive/Getty Images; p. 23 George Pimental/WireImage/Getty Images; pp. 29, 35 Alexander Joe/AFP/Getty Images; p. 31 Tony Karumba/AFP/Getty Images; p. 40 Kirk McKoy/Los Angeles Times/Getty Images; p. 42 © AF Archive/Alamy Sto ck Photo; pp. 45, 46 Marco Longari/AFP/Getty Images; back cover, pp. 8, 17, 25, 47 (skulls) rangizzz/Shutterstock.com; pp. 7, 13, 23, 36, 44 (top) pimchawee/Shutterstock.com; additional background textures Reinhold Leitner/ Shutterstock.com, © iStockphoto.com/ShutterWorx

Designer: Brian Garvey; Photo Researcher: Heather Moore Niver